101 TIPS for Preschool Teachers

Creating Theme Environments

By Barbara F. Backer
Illustrated by Priscilla Burris

Warren Publishing House
A Division of Frank Schaffer Publications
Torrance, California

Dedicated with love to my son,
Sam Backer, who discovers the joy of life
in every environment and spreads
that joy wherever he goes.

— *B. F. B.*

Managing Editor: Kathleen Cubley
Editor: Susan Hodges
Contributing Editors: Gayle Bittinger, Elizabeth McKinnon, Jean Warren
Copyeditor: Kris Fulsaas
Proofreader: Mae Rhodes
Editorial Assistant: Durby Peterson
Graphic Designer: Sarah Ness
Graphic Designer (cover): Brenda Mann Harrison
Layout Artist: Gordon Frazier
Production Managers: Jo Anna Haffner, Melody Olney

ISBN: 1-57029-092-X

Printed in the United States of America
Published by Warren Publishing House
    Editorial Office: P.O. Box 2250
                         Everett, WA 98203
    Sales Office: 23740 Hawthorne Blvd.
                         Torrance, CA 90505

20 19 18 17 16 15 14 13 12 11 10 9 8 7 6 5 4 3 2 1

Contents

Dinosaur Days 4

Farm................................... 6

Circus 8

Outer Space........................... 10

Polar Regions 12

Desert................................. 14

Ranch 16

Pond 18

The Seashore........................... 20

Under the Sea.......................... 22

Dinosaur Days

Dinosaurs fascinate children. The huge beasts spark imagination and breathe excitement into learning. Create an environment where dinosaurs are free to roam in children's imaginations and where dinosaur activities bring history to life.

1 Hang a huge dinosaur banner outside your door with a sign reading, "The Land of Dinosaurs." Banners are commercially available, or your children can make one by painting a huge dinosaur that you've sketched on a bed sheet. To give the feeling of a prehistoric environment, hang paper vines from the top of the door frame so the children will pass through the vines as they enter the room.

2 Discuss plants that lived when the dinosaurs lived. Bring several varieties of ferns to show your children. Let them examine the plants with a magnifying glass. Encourage them to compare and contrast the different plants.

If vines grow nearby, bring some in, or take the children to see them. You can also make vines by cutting ³/₄-inch-wide strips of brown or black paper. Have your children attach green paper leaves to both sides of each strip. Hang different lengths of vines from your room's ceiling.

3 Have your children make a dinosaur mural. Help them brainstorm about what they want to include and how they could make those things. Together, look at picture-book illustrations for ideas. For instance, your children could fingerpaint a background and use dinosaur-shaped sponges to make prints on the foreground. Tissue paper leaves and real twigs add to the fun.

4 Let your children be paleontologists for a day. Hide chicken bones around your room for your children to discover. (Disinfect the bones beforehand by boiling them for 20 minutes, then soaking them overnight in a 10 percent bleach solution.) Have the children glue their finds to a paper dinosaur shape.

5 Set up a dinosaur museum. Invite your children to bring toy dinosaurs from home to put on display, or to exhibit dinosaurs they've sculpted from clay. Label all items with the dinosaur's name and the contributor's name. Let the children help make the labels. Accept all attempts, from scribbles and invented spelling to copied words.

6 Children enjoy moving like dinosaurs to music. Any plodding music works well. "Bydlo" from Moussorgsky's *Pictures at an Exhibition* and "Fossils" from Saint-Saens' *Carnival of the Animals* are good choices.

7 Songs such as the following one engage children's imaginations.

Sung to: "If I Had a Hammer"

If I had a dinosaur,
I'd ride it in the morning.
I'd ride it in the evening,
All over this land.
We'd climb up mountains,
And slide down into valleys,
And sing this happy song all day long,
All over this land.

Barbara Backer

8 Extend this theme to the sand table by putting plastic dinosaurs in the sand. Your children will find ways to add swamps and other features. Have them create more dinosaurs, plants, volcanoes, and other items from paper, boxes, glue, and other art materials. All can become part of the sand table environment.

9 Together, make a huge stuffed dinosaur. Cut two identical dinosaur paper shapes, taller than your children, out of butcher paper. Lay one on top of the other and mark the "inside" and "outside" of each. Have your children paint the outside. Next, have them spread glue around the edges of one unpainted side, leaving openings at the top and bottom. Lay the second dinosaur on top of the first, and seal the glued edges. Have the children fill the dinosaur shape with crumpled newspaper and glue it shut. Lean your creation against a wall or hang it from the ceiling so its feet just touch the floor.

10 Children better understand fossil remains when they create their own. Show them how to make fossil imprints by pressing plastic dinosaurs into modeling dough.

Farm

If at all possible, take a trip to a working farm to see how vegetables grow and to observe farm animals close-up. Watch the farmer milk a cow or a goat, and let your children have a turn, too. When you return to your room, dig into these farm-related activities.

1 Decorate your door to look like a barn door. If you have room, cut a large barn shape from butcher paper and attach it around the door. Add a sign: "Welcome to Our Farm."

2 Decorate your room with several bales of hay. You can get these at a feed store. Put work gloves, overalls, boots, straw hats, and plastic fruits and vegetables in the dramatic play center. To extend the mood, try wearing overalls and a straw hat!

3 Place a toy barn, plastic animals, and toy pickup trucks and tractors in the block center. Add empty oatmeal containers for silos and blue or brown fabric for a pond. Wooden cubes or spools and plastic-foam chips can be loaded on trucks and wagons. Shredded paper can be hay for the animals.

4 Have your children work together to make a scarecrow. Brainstorm to decide what you will need and how you will go about making one. It's fun to make several scarecrows so everyone has a greater opportunity to be involved, so how about creating a scarecrow family? Discuss the scarecrow's job on the farm. What other ways might farmers protect their crops?

5 Sing "Old MacDonald Had a Farm" together. After the usual verses, ask your children what else Farmer MacDonald might have had on his farm. A TV? A teddy bear? Red pajamas? Encourage creative thinking. Now sing the song again. Ask each child in turn to suggest a new verse.

Later, have your children make a group book about Old MacDonald's Farm. Let each child make one page of the book by drawing a picture of something Old MacDonald had on his farm. (Accept all answers. Unusual responses add humor to the song.) Add words, and gather the pages into a book. The children will enjoy following the book as they sing the song.

6 Make a farm scene on the wall. Discuss what is found on the farm. Then set out precut shapes of these items for your children to decorate. (Older children can draw and cut out their own.) Have your children glue their creations to the mural. Increase interest by adding other textures to the scene. Craft sticks make good fences, and holograph gift-wrap works well as a pond with sunshine reflecting from it. Label the board: "Old MacDonald's Farm," or any name the children choose. Label parts of the scene as you wish.

7 Use die-cut paper animal shapes to make math games. Write one numeral (0 to 9) on each of ten shapes. Cover the shapes with clear self-stick paper. Ask your children to place the shapes in numerical order, or to "feed the animals" by putting the corresponding number of kernels of dried corn on each animal.

These animal shapes can be used with songs, as well. Using a variety of animal shapes, distribute one shape to each child. As you sing "Old MacDonald Had a Farm," have the children hold up the animal mentioned in each verse and make that animal's sound.

8 To show the variety of things that come from farms, make a display of farm-produced items. Cover a table with a farm print or vegetable print fabric. Put out fresh and canned fruits and vegetables, empty milk cartons, egg cartons, cottage cheese containers, bread wrappers, wool clothing, and other items. Discuss the items and how they relate to farms. Sort and classify the items together.

9 Look for pictures of farm animals in discarded books and magazines and in parent-teacher stores. Illustrated brochures on farming are available from your county cooperative extension office. Mount these pictures on heavy paper and use them for an assortment of activities.

10 Fill your room with the aroma of fruits and vegetables while your children prepare each day's snack. Ask each child to bring in a piece of fresh fruit. Have the children wash and cut the fruit to make fruit salad. Use plastic knives with serrated blades for safe cutting. On another day, have children wash and tear lettuce for a green salad.

Circus

Children of all ages love the circus, and this environment leads to learning about people, occupations, animals, physical feats, and more. Turn your room into a circus arena, and let the show begin.

1 Start this unit with a bare room—just as the arena is bare when the circus arrives in town. As your children learn about the circus, show them circus pictures and posters, and then have them make posters and pennants to decorate the room. Place their posters and some balloons on your door, or decorate the door with pictures of clowns and a sign reading, "Clowns Inside."

2 Decorate your room with paper chains and crepe-paper streamers. Drape them from the center of the ceiling to the place where the ceiling meets the walls. Leave a little extra to hang down the wall a foot or two. With enough chains and streamers, your room will be transformed into a circus tent.

3 Hang a trapeze from your ceiling, with a rag doll or stuffed animal attached. Paint a dowel and tie rope to each end of it for the trapeze. Use yarn, twine, or tape to attach the performer to the trapeze.

4 Transform your snack center into a concession stand. Have children make paper money to spend. One day serve popcorn in paper cups; another day have the children make lemonade to sell to each other. The children can make snow cones by pouring fruit juice over scooped, shaved ice. Offer several choices of juice.

5 Fill your reading area with picture books about the circus. Nonfiction books for children and adults are full of realistic pictures. Find books on circus history that show how the circus used to be, with elephants putting up tents and circus wagons pulled by horses.

9 Culminate your unit of study with a circus. Have your children make their own costumes and sit in a circle (the ring). Have one or more ringmasters announce each act. (Offer your ring-masters help as needed.) Let animal trainers tame the wild beasts, acrobats perform routines, and clowns do their silly stunts. Children are more relaxed if they perform only for each other, so resist the temptation to invite others and make this a big production.

10 Ringling Bros. and Barnum & Bailey Circus distributes free curriculum materials to class-room teachers. Send a postcard with your name and address to the following address.

Ringling Bros. and Barnum & Bailey Circus
8607 Westwood Center Drive
Vienna, VA 22182
Attention: Educational department

6 Invite your children to bring stuffed animals to school to perform in your circus. Encourage the children to work in pairs or small groups to devise tricks for the animals to perform. Later, they can sort the animals or arrange them by size.

7 Take this theme outside. Decorate playground equipment with crepe-paper or fabric streamers. Put Hula Hoops on the ground for circus rings. Decorate riding toys for clowns to use. Paint large cardboard cartons as clown houses or cars, and cut doors and windows. Bring a tape player outside and provide circus music while your children play.

8 Show your children how to make circus costumes from one or two simple props. A child wearing a striped shirt and a yarn tail becomes a tiger. The one in a leotard or tutu is a trapeze artist. A high hat and a megaphone are all you need to become ringmaster, and a funny hat and a bit of makeup transform you into a clown.

Outer Space

Outer space is dark and quiet. When people travel there, they float, moving slowly in their weightless state. It sounds like a teacher's dream environment! Transform your room into a space scene, and remind your children to float quietly when they move around the room.

1 Spread dark butcher paper on the floor, and invite your children to make a space mural. (Cover surrounding areas, and put smocks on the children to protect them from flying paint.) Show your children how to dip a brush in paint and flick their wrist to make a spatter design on the paper. Use several colors of paint to create a vibrant night sky. When this dries, it becomes the background paper for your mural.

2 Display your space background on the wall at your children's eye level. Have the children add self-stick stars and triangle and rectangle shapes cut from holograph gift-wrap or aluminum foil. Let them glue these to the background paper to make rocket ships.

3 Post a space rhyme, such as the following one, near your display. Help your children learn the words and encourage them to act out the rhyme with creative movement.

I want to be an astronaut
And fly up to the moon.
I'll soar around the Milky Way
And won't come back 'til June.

Barbara Backer

4 Stimulate your children to build space constructions by putting pictures of planets, space stations, and satellites in the block center. Show the children how to make silvery building blocks by wrapping aluminum foil around blocks or oatmeal boxes.

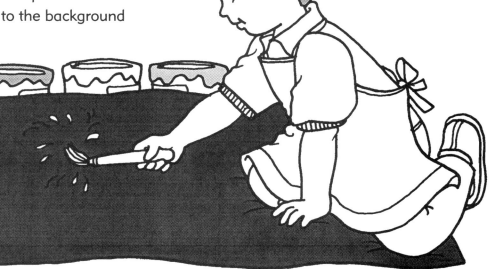

7 Have your children make space stations by gluing empty boxes and cartons together. When the glue dries, they can paint their creations or wrap them with aluminum foil. Children can work alone or in pairs or small groups. Place the completed creations around the room. Hang some from the ceiling as if in orbit.

8 Fill your room with astronauts. Trace around each child's body on butcher paper. Cut out the resulting figures. Have your children draw in their facial features. Suggest that they also color the feet and hands to look like boots and gloves, and add buttons, gauges, and hoses to the body to make it look like a space suit. Hang the figures from the ceiling with thread. Hang some upside down, and hang some by their feet or by their sides so all appear weightless.

9 Fill your reading area with fiction and nonfiction books about space. Books written for older children have wonderful pictures for little ones.

5 Add "spacewear" to your dramatic play area. Apply reflective tape to oversize T-shirts to make costumes. Helmets can be as simple as aluminum colanders, or they can be made by cutting the bottom and side from a gallon bleach bottle. You can also make a helmet by cutting a hole (face shield) in the side of a cardboard ice cream tub.

6 Make satellites to hang from the ceiling. Have your children paint round wooden toothpicks with white tempera paint. Dry these on waxed paper overnight. The following day, the children can poke the toothpicks into plastic-foam balls.

10 Decorate a sweatshirt or T-shirt to wear while your children study space. Cut star shapes from gold and silver fabric. Use fusible webbing to appliqué these to a dark shirt. Outline the stars with glittery fabric paint. Clerks in a fabric or craft shop can show you this easy process in a few minutes.

Polar Regions

The Arctic and Antarctic regions seem barren, but many animals and plants live there. The polar regions are fun to study in summer or winter. Add excitement by having your children prepare for a make-believe expedition.

1 Place a "Polar Expeditions" sign on your door. Write each child's name on a small pennant shape and arrange these near the sign. Display pictures of Arctic animals on one side of the room and Antarctic animals on the other.

Have your children talk about an "expedition" and what explorers need to take along. Put sunglasses, warm hats, boots, parkas, and other props in the dramatic play center. Provide discarded cameras (without film) so explorers can photograph their discoveries, and clipboards and pens so they can write reports.

2 Place some small pillows on a table and drape a white sheet over all to simulate snow and icy ground. Drape blue scarves over part of this for water. Have your children fashion polar animals from modeling dough to put in the display. Add vinyl animals and fish. Challenge your children to think of other things to add and ways to make them.

3 Use pictures of polar animals for graphing activities. Help your children categorize the animals according to color, number of legs, or other characteristics.

4 Cut easel paper in the shapes of polar animals. The cut paper can be used for other activities. Record stories of whales on whale-shaped paper and descriptions of penguins on penguin-shaped paper.

5 Polar animals move in strange and wonderful ways. For instance, the penguin is a flightless bird. Seals, so sleek and graceful in the water, lumber awkwardly on land with only their flippers to propel them. Polar bears are powerful swimmers with giant paws for sure footing on the ice. Have your children imitate these and other polar creatures as you play "The Skater's Waltz" or other instrumental music.

8 It's easy to show children how camouflage protects animals. Give your children precut polar animal shapes. (Older children may want to cut out their own.) Animals that are always white or that turn white for the winter should be cut from white paper. Other animals should be cut from colored paper or colored by the children. Have the children glue their shapes to white paper. Then have them view the creation from a distance. What do they see?

9 Put molded vinyl polar animals in your block center or water table. Sets (available from parent-teacher stores) include polar bears, penguins, whales, and more. In the water table, challenge children to construct ice and land for the land animals. Offer milk jugs, plastic bottles and other containers for their use. Help the children brainstorm how they can create a polar environment in the block center. Offer scarves, fabric, and cotton batting.

6 Simulate icebergs in the water table. Freeze water in a variety of plastic containers, large and small. Float the resulting ice shapes in the water table. Provide terry towels and basins of warm water to heat your children's hands after they play in the icy water.

7 Add a freezing touch to a matching game. Freeze water in a variety of small, medium, and large plastic containers. Include small and extra-large margarine tubs and 1-, 2-, and 3-quart plastic bowls. Unmold the ice onto cafeteria trays and have your children match each ice block to its mold. They'll play with these for hours, and will enjoy predicting which ice blocks will melt first and last.

10 Fill your reading area with books about the geography, plants, and animals of polar regions.

Desert

There are deserts around the world. It's best to pick one area to discuss, and these suggestions are based on animals and plants in the Sonoran Desert of the southwestern United States. Use these tips to help you re-create the desert in your room.

1 Have your children make a desert scene as a large mural or a bulletin board. This is a week-long project. Begin by having the children paint the background. For a mottled, sunbleached, or moon-kissed look, dip small oval sponges into tempera paint. Press these to the background paper in a random pattern using sky tones on the upper half of the paper and earth tones below. Put sand in the earth-tone paints to add texture to the mural. Since most desert animals stay hidden during the hot daylight hours, consider making a nighttime scene that includes nocturnal animals and night-blooming plants.

2 As your children learn about desert plants and animals, have them glue cutouts of these flora and fauna to the mural. If desired, the children can color them first. Glue some of the figures to small pieces of cardboard and then to the mural to make them stick out from the surface. Cut cactus shapes from corrugated cardboard. Have the children paint them green, then add small tissue paper flowers. Together, look in books and at nature videos for other ideas.

3 Children like to play with rubber stamps. Look for rubber stamps of desert plants and animals, including desert flowers, saguaro cacti, coyotes, snakes, and owls. Your children can use the stamps to decorate the mural, and you can use them to make learning games.

4 Children are captivated by the unusual, so they really like learning about the large saguaro cactus. Native to the Americas, it is actually a tree. Give your children large sheets of green paper cut into saguaro cactus shapes. Let them glue broken toothpicks to the paper for prickly cactus spines. Hang the completed pictures around your room to surround your learning area with these gentle giants.

5 Bring several types of cacti, including some that blossom, into the room. Use these real cacti for math activities. Have your children arrange them in order by height, or sort them into two categories: those that are blooming and those that are not.

8 Put desert animal puppets or stuffed animals in the language center. Place plastic animals in the sand table and the block center. Encourage your children to make cacti from green modeling dough to add to the sand table or block center.

9 Cut cactus shapes from green felt. Write a number (0 to 5, or 0 to 10) on each. Cut small flower shapes. Put cactus and flowers at the flannelboard. Have your children put the correct number of flowers on each cactus.

10 Become part of the desert environment. Purchase or decorate a T-shirt or sweatshirt to wear while teaching about the desert. Wildlife organizations have many attractive shirts available. To decorate your own, select a beige shirt. Cut a saguaro cactus shape from green fabric and attach the shape to the shirt with fusible webbing. Outline the cactus shape with green fabric paint. (Get directions and supplies at a fabric or craft store.)

6 Take the opportunity to explore and discuss texture with your children. Have the children examine the prickly surface of a cactus with a magnifying glass. Let them gently touch the plant's sharp spines. Use the word *prickly* to describe the cactus. Then play the following game.

Gather some prickly items, like a brush, a pine cone, and a plastic fork. Place them in a container with a variety of soft items, like a mitten, a stuffed animal, and a cotton ball. Let your children sort the items according to their texture.

7 Use a copy machine with enlarging and reducing capabilities to make several sizes of cactus or animal pictures. Use these as patterns for flannelboard figures. Have your children place the figures on the flannelboard in order from smallest to largest (or largest to smallest). Cut out same-size figures, too, for patterning activities.

Ranch

Ranch life and ranch workers captivate the imagination of young children. But cowpokes are real people whose protective clothing and unique tools enable them to do the hard work necessary to raise livestock. As your children study ranch life, they'll learn to respect these workers and value their work in a new way.

1 Cover your door with butcher paper. Have your children decide on a name for the group's ranch, and write "Welcome to the _____ Ranch" on the butcher paper. Provide precut cowboy, horse, and cattle figures for the children to color and glue to the paper. (Older children can draw and cut out their own figures.)

2 Western-wear catalogs are filled with pictures of people in cowboy garb. Send for a few of these catalogs before you begin your ranch unit. You can use the pictures for flannelboard stories, art projects, learning games, and many other activities.

3 Buy or cut out paper boot and hat shapes to use for matching and patterning games.

4 Ask your children to bring in yardsticks. Provide extras for children who forget. Give the children precut horse head shapes. (Older children can draw and cut out their own.) Have the children decorate the heads with markers or crayons. They can glue on yarn snips for a mane, if desired. With glue or masking tape, attach each head to the end of a yardstick to make a hobby horse. The children can "ride" their horses indoors or out.

5 Cattle brands, with their distinctive symbols, can be the basis for a variety of activities. Display pictures of cattle brands in your writing area for your children to copy. Challenge the children to create their own cattle brands. What do the symbols mean? Make a set of cattle brand cards for use in matching and memory games.

6 Include props such as bandannas, cowboy hats, vests, a sheriff's badge, a frying pan, cooking utensils, a canteen, rope, and hobby horses in your dramatic play center.

7 Cowboys like to sing. Write this song on a chart and point to the words as your children sing. Let the children take turns wearing a cowboy hat and leading the group. The leader makes a motion, and the children copy the motion while everyone sings. The leader gives the hat to another child, who becomes the next leader.

Sung to: "Did You Ever See a Lassie?"

Did you ever see a cowboy,
A cowboy, a cowboy?
Did you ever see a cowboy
Go this way and that?
Go this way and that way?
Go that way and this way?
Did you ever see a cowboy
Go this way and that?

Repeat the song for each child, substituting *cowgirl* for *cowboy* as necessary.

Barbara Backer

8 Snacks are a must on the hot, dusty trail. Set out several different kinds of dried fruit, seeds, and cereal pieces, each in a separate bowl. Select a large plastic bag and let each of your children scoop an ingredient into it. Shake the bag thoroughly to mix. Have each cowpoke remove a scoop of the finished mix and put it into his or her own zippered sandwich bag for nourishment on the trail (or playground).

9 Because clothesline is thick but soft, it's easy to untie knots in it. Cut several lengths of line. Dip half of each length into diluted food coloring; remove, and dry. The different-colored ends help your children see what happens when they tie knots. All of this tying and untying develops fine motor skills.

10 Cut cowboy and cowgirl figures from felt for use on the flannelboard. Include felt hats, jackets, vests, boots, and other clothing items. Let your children take turns dressing the figures, naming each article of clothing as they put it on.

Pond

Whether located in a national forest, in a local park, or at the back of a shopping center, ponds are marvelous habitats that are rich in plant and animal life. There are many small animals to investigate and lots of intriguing flying and swimming insects. Bring the pond environment into your room with these tips.

1 Take your children to see a real pond, if possible. Discuss the animals and plants you see there. Which are in the water and which are on the shore? Then work together to create a pond scene in your room. Draw a large oval for a pond at the bottom corner of a piece of white butcher paper. Have your children add a sky and shore to this scene. They can glue small pieces of blue and green tissue paper to the pond for water. Cattails and other grasses can be painted with cotton swabs, and animals can be sponge-painted at the water's edge. (Look for animal sponges at parent-teacher and craft stores.) Real leaves and twigs add to the environment. Encourage your children to contribute their ideas.

2 Have your children name the parts of the pond mural. Help them make a label for each part.

3 There are many colorful fabrics with prints of pond animals and flowers. These can be used in many ways: to cover bulletin boards, doors, and tables; as blankets and costumes for dramatic play; or as a work surface for the block center. You can cut figures from these fabrics to use as appliqués for a T-shirt, a sweatshirt, or an apron.

4 Bring the pond to the flannelboard. Cut five felt frog shapes of various sizes. Have your children arrange them in order from smallest to largest. Cut out a log and a "pond" shape. Put the frogs on the log and count the frogs as the children sing "Five Little Speckled Frogs" or another counting song.

5 It's fun to move like pond animals. Hopping frogs and toads, darting dragonflies, slithering snakes, and quacking ducks delight young children. Take movement activities outdoors when weather permits.

6 Turn your water table into a simulated pond. Put models of pond animals in the water. Add real leaves and twigs, and float plastic ducks on top.

9 Children love to go fishing in a make-believe pond. To make a fishing pole, string a small magnet from the end of a wooden dowel. Cut fish shapes from various colors of construction paper. Put a paper clip on the nose of each fish. To make a pond, spread a blue towel on the floor and scatter the fish on it. Let your children take turns dipping the pole into the pond. While one child fishes, the remaining children can sing the following song.

Sung to: "The Farmer in the Dell"

I can catch a fish.
I can catch a fish.
Put in my line, and I'll do fine.
I can catch a fish.

Barbara Backer

7 Float water lilies in your water-table pond. To make the flowers, cut two individual cups from a plastic-foam egg carton. Cut each section into a lily shape. Put one inside the other and push a brass paper fastener through the bottom of the blossom to attach it to a base cut from a plastic-foam food tray.

8 Bring an empty plastic wading pool into your room, along with a few plastic fish, frogs, and plants. Your children will spend hours playing in this "pond," and they may even think of new accessories to add.

10 Help your children take a survey to discover which is your group's favorite pond animal. Have them narrow the field to two or three candidates. Make a chart with a column for each animal. Draw or glue a picture of each animal to the top of its column. Have each child make a mark in one column to vote for his or her favorite. Tally the votes and discuss the results.

The Seashore

The edge of the sea draws people with its beauty and its magical qualities. What is seen one hour may not be there the next. The shore is always changing. Help your children learn to love the shore and its beauty, and teach them the value of preserving the beach.

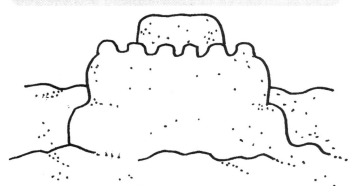

1 Children (and adults) love to build sand castles. Put plastic containers of various shapes and sizes in the outdoor sandbox and the indoor sand table. Dampen the sand so it will hold its shape. Show your children how to pack damp sand into the containers and then unmold it. Display pictures of sand castles to inspire young builders.

2 Beachcombing is part of the fun of a trip to the shore. Bury seashells in your sand area or hide them around the room for your children to discover. Set a few shells in your Water Table for the children to brush clean.

3 Put out a dishpan full of seashells for your children to explore. Encourage the children to sort the shells, arrange them from largest to smallest or from darkest to lightest, use them for patterning, match them to numerals, and more.

4 The surf rubs holes in some seashells. Put these in the art center for painting and stringing into necklaces and bracelets.

5 Together, create a seashore mural or a bulletin board display. Add sand to the paint for the shore. Provide real seashells for gluing along the sand. Encourage your children to add pictures of sea animals and birds to the display.

6 Craft stores and parent-teacher stores sell sponges cut into shapes of shells and seashore animals. Purchase a few (or cut your own from a plain kitchen sponge). Use them for sponge-painting critters directly onto the mural, or have the children print them onto easel paper, then continue painting at the easel.

9 Set up a terrarium for hermit crabs (available at pet stores) and display them in your room. Your children can take turns feeding them and changing their water. Put empty shells in the terrarium and watch to see which shells the crabs select to live in as they grow.

10 Make a bottle full of ocean waves for your children to play with. Fill a plastic soda bottle two-thirds full with water tinted with blue food coloring. Fill the bottle to the top with mineral oil, leaving no air in the bottle. Screw the bottle securely shut, sealing it with glue, and wrap the cap with duct tape to discourage the children from trying to open it. Check the bottle daily to be certain the duct tape is tightly sealed. To create waves, hold the bottle on its side and gently rock it back and forth.

7 Children are surprised to learn that huge turtles live in the ocean. These animals come onto shore to lay their eggs. Have your children make turtles to place around the room. Turn a paper bowl upside down, and paint it for the turtle's shell. Cut out feet, a head, and a tail from construction paper and glue them in place.

8 Put a few beach chairs and a beach umbrella in your language center to transform it into a sunny beach. Include props such as a beach towel, sunglasses, a beach hat, empty sunscreen bottles, sports drink bottles, sandals, and a few magazines in a beach bag. Display books about the seashore in this center.

Under the Sea

There is more water than land on Earth, and the largest bodies of water are the oceans. They are full of plant and animal life. Transform your room into an underwater wonderland while you learn about life under the sea. Plan to spend several weeks on this project.

1 Cover the ceiling with blue paper, the windows with blue plastic food wrap, and tables with underwater-print fabric. Have your children decorate the room with paper fish and other sea creatures. Show your children how to make translucent jellyfish by squirting blobs of white glue onto waxed paper, then sprinkling a bit of glitter on the glue. Let these dry several days, until clear. Peel off the waxed paper, punch a hole in each shape, and add a loop of thread for hanging.

2 Make a huge stuffed shark or whale, using the method described on page 5 (tip 9). Hang this from the ceiling or prop it against a wall. Make other stuffed fish and hang them on walls around the room, or pile them in the corners of each center like schools of fish gathered in dark areas of the ocean. Your children will use them in dramatic play.

3 Make a gigantic aquarium mural. Let your children add to the display as they learn new things about underwater life. First, have children make finger-paintings using blues, greens, violets, and yellows. Hang these close together to make the background of an underwater mural. Cut sponges into fish shapes and let your children sponge-paint fishes on the mural. Add underwater plants made from twisted green crepe-paper streamers. If desired, decorate a cereal box to resemble a pirate chest, and glue it to the board.

4 Your children can make octopuses by cutting two matching oval shapes from colored butcher paper. Glue the edges of the ovals together to make a pouch. Stuff the pouch with crumpled tissue paper before sealing it. Glue eight strips of tissue paper (in matching colors) to the back. If these octopuses are small enough, glue them to your mural. If not, punch a hole in the top of each octopus and hang these creatures from the ceiling.

8 Include underwater delicacies for snack. Offer children tastes of tuna, mackerel, sardines, shrimp, clams, fish sticks, or other fish. Invite families to share their favorite fish dishes with you.

9 Your children can create underwater pictures of brightly colored plants and fish. Have them use fluorescent crayons to draw their underwater scenes. Remind them to push hard on the crayons for good coverage. Next they brush on a coat of thinned blue or blue-purple tempera paint. The paint won't adhere to heavily waxed crayon surfaces, so fish and seaweed seem to move in water.

5 Ask each of your children to draw his or her favorite sea creature. Mount these drawings on fish-shaped paper, and compile them into a group book. You can easily turn this into a repetitive rhyme in the style of Bill Martin's *Brown Bear, Brown Bear, What Do You See?* (Holt, 1983). As you turn each page, incorporate the picture into the rhyme. For example, "Gray whale, gray whale, what do you see? I see a yellow fish looking at me."

10 Set up an aquarium of tropical fish in your room. Learn the names and characteristics of each of your fish. Include scavenger fish who help keep the tank clean. Let your children help select the fish, and put clipboards of drawing paper with crayons near the tank so the children can draw what they see.

6 Bring in natural sponges for your children to explore. Use some for painting. Put some in the water table and others in the dramatic play area so the children can use them to wash their dishes.

7 Invite a scuba diver to visit your group and demonstrate the equipment used underwater. Have your visitor tell about what is seen under the water. Let your children try on goggles and fins.

TIP 101

Use Totline® Resources

When you need ideas for helping young children learn and grow, turn to Totline Publications. Our books are quality, classroom-tested resources for teachers, directors, daycare providers, parents, and others who work with children ages 2 to 6. The innovative ideas presented in our materials challenge and engage young children but

need only minimal preparation and common, inexpensive materials. Totline Publications makes learning fun for everyone.